GW00728047

SHOOTING NIAGARA:

AND AFTER?

BY

THOMAS CARLYLE.

Reprinted from *Macmillan's Magazine for August* 1867.
With some Additions and Corrections.

LONDON:
CHAPMAN AND HALL, 193 PICCADILLY.
1867.

SHOOTING NIAGARA: AND AFTER?

I.

THERE probably never was since the Heptarchy ended, or almost since it began, so hugely critical an epoch in the history of England as this we have now entered upon, with universal self-congratulation and flinging up of caps; nor one in which,—with no Norman Invasion now ahead, to lay hold of it, to bridle and regulate it for us (little thinking it was *for us*), and guide it into higher and wider regions,—the question of utter death or of nobler new life for the poor Country was so uncertain. Three things seem to be agreed upon by gods and men, at least by English men and gods; certain to happen, and are now in visible course of fulfilment.

1° *Democracy* to complete itself; to go the full length of its course, towards the Bottomless or into it, no power now extant to prevent it or even considerably retard it, —till we have seen where it will lead us to, and whether there will *then* be any return possible, or none. Complete "liberty" to all persons; Count of Heads to be the Divine Court of Appeal on every question and interest of mankind; Count of Heads to choose a Parliament according to its own heart at last, and sit with Penny Newspapers zealously watching the same; said Parliament, so chosen and so watched, to do what trifle of legislating and administering may still be needed in

B

such an England, with its hundred and fifty millions
'free' more and more to follow each his own nose, by
way of guide-post in this intricate world.

2° That, in a limited time, say fifty years hence, the
Church, all Churches and so-called religions, the Christian Religion itself, shall have deliquesced,—into "Liberty of Conscience," Progress of Opinion, Progress of
Intellect, Philanthropic Movement, and other aqueous
residues, of a vapid badly scented character;—and shall,
like water spilt upon the ground, trouble nobody considerably thenceforth, but evaporate at its leisure.

3° That, in lieu thereof, there shall be Free Trade,
in all senses, and to all lengths: unlimited Free Trade,
—which some take to mean, 'Free racing, ere long with
unlimited speed, in the career of *Cheap and Nasty;'*—
this beautiful career, not in shop-goods only, but in all
things temporal, spiritual and eternal, to be flung ge-
nerously open, wide as the portals of the Universe; so
that everybody shall start free, and everywhere, 'under
enlightened popular suffrage,' the race shall be to the
swift, and the high office shall fall to him who is ablest
if not to do it, at least to get elected for doing it.

These are three altogether new and very considerable achievements, lying visibly ahead of us, not far off,
—and so extremely considerable, that every thinking
English creature is tempted to go into manifold reflections and inquiries upon them. My own have not been
wanting, any time these thirty years past, but they have
not been of a joyful or triumphant nature; not prone to
utter themselves; indeed expecting, till lately, that they
might with propriety lie unuttered altogether. But the
series of events comes swifter and swifter, at a strange
rate; and hastens unexpectedly,—'velocity increasing'
(if you will consider, for this too is as when the little

stone has been loosened, which sets the whole mountain-
side in motion) 'as the *square* of the time :'—so that the
wisest Prophecy finds it was quite wrong as to date;
and, patiently, or even indolently waiting, is astonished
to see itself fulfilled, not in centuries as anticipated, but
in decades and years. It was a clear prophecy, for instance, that Germany would either become honourably
Prussian or go to gradual annihilation: but who of us
expected that we ourselves, instead of our children's
children, should live to behold it; that a magnanimous
and fortunate Herr von Bismarck, whose dispraise was
in all the Newspapers, would, to his own amazement,
find the thing now doable; and would do it, do the
essential of it, in a few of the current weeks? That
England would have to take the Niagara leap of com-
pleted Democracy one day, was also a plain prophecy,
though uncertain as to time.

II.

The prophecy, truly, was plain enough this long
while :—" Δόγμα γὰρ αὐτῶν τίς μεταβάλλει; For who
can change the opinion of these people!" as the sage
Antoninus notes. It is indeed strange how prepposses-
sions and delusions seize upon whole communities of
men; no basis in the notion they have formed, yet
everybody adopting it, everybody finding the whole
world agree with him in it, and accept it as an axiom
of Euclid; and, in the universal repetition and reverberation, taking all contradiction of it as an insult, and
a sign of malicious insanity, hardly to be borne with
patience. "For who can change the opinion of these
people?" as our Divus Imperator says. No wisest of
mortals. This people cannot be convinced out of its

" axiom of Euclid" by any reasoning whatsoever; on the contrary, all the world assenting, and continually repeating and reverberating, there soon comes that singular phenomenon, which the Germans call *Schwärmerey* ('*enthusiasm*' is our poor Greek equivalent), which means simply '*Swarmery*,' or the 'Gathering of Men in Swarms,' and what prodigies they are in the habit of doing and believing, when thrown into that miraculous condition.   Some big Queen Bee is in the centre of the swarm; but any commonplace stupidest *bee*, Cleon the Tanner, Beales, John of Leyden, John of Bromwicham, any bee whatever, if he can happen, by noise or otherwise, to be chosen for the function, will straightway get fatted and inflated into *bulk*, which of itself means complete capacity; no difficulty about your Queen Bee : and the swarm once formed, finds itself impelled to action, as with one heart and one mind.   Singular, in the case of human swarms, with what perfection of unanimity and quasi-religious conviction the stupidest absurdities can be received as axioms of Euclid, nay as articles of faith, which you are not only to believe, unless malignantly insane, but are (if you have any honour or morality) to push into practice, and without delay see *done*, if your soul would live !   Divine commandment *to vote* ("Manhood Suffrage,"— Horsehood, Doghood ditto not yet treated of); universal "glorious Liberty" (to Sons of the Devil in overwhelming majority, as would appear); count of Heads the God-appointed way in this Universe, all other ways Devil-appointed; in one brief word, which includes whatever of palpable incredibility and delirious absurdity, universally believed, can be uttered or imagined on these points, "the equality of men," any man equal to any other; Quashee Nigger to Socrates or Shakspeare; Judas Iscariot to Jesus Christ;

—and Bedlam and Gehenna equal to the New Jerusalem, shall we say? If these things are taken up, not only as axioms of Euclid, but as articles of religion burning to be put in practice for the salvation of the world,—I think you will admit that *Swarmery* plays a wonderful part in the heads of poor Mankind; and that very considerable results are likely to follow from it in our day!

But you will in vain attempt, by argument of human intellect, to contradict or turn aside any of these divine axioms, indisputable as those of Euclid, and of sacred or quasi-celestial quality to boot: if you have neglected the one method (which was a silent one) of dealing with them at an early stage, they are thenceforth invincible; and will plunge more and more madly forward towards practical fulfilment. Once fulfilled, it will then be seen how credible and wise they were. Not even the Queen Bee but will then know what to think of them. Then, and never till then.

By far the notablest case of *Swarmery,* in these times, is that of the late American War, with Settlement of the Nigger Question for result. Essentially the Nigger Question was one of the smallest; and in itself did not much concern mankind in the present time of struggles and hurries. One always rather likes the Nigger; evidently a poor blockhead with good dispositions, with affections, attachments,—with a turn for Nigger Melodies, and the like:—he is the only Savage of all the coloured races that doesn't die out on sight of the White Man; but can actually live beside him, and work and increase and be merry. The Almighty Maker has appointed him to be a Servant. Under penalty of Heaven's curse, neither party to this

pre-appointment shall neglect or misdo his duties
therein ;—and it is certain (though as yet widely unknown), Servantship on the nomadic principle, at the
rate of so many shillings per day, *cannot* be other than
misdone.   The whole world rises in shrieks against you,
on hearing of such a thing:—yet the whole world,
listening to those cool Sheffield disclosures of *rattening*,
and the market-rates of murder in that singular 'Sheffield Assassination Company (Limited),' feels its hair
rising on end;—to little purpose hitherto; being without even a gallows to make response!   The fool of a
world listens, year after year, for above a generation
back, to " disastrous *strikes*," " merciless *lockouts*," and
other details of the nomadic scheme of servitude; nay
is becoming thoroughly disquieted about its own too
lofty-minded flunkeys, mutinous maid-servants (ending,
naturally enough, as " distressed needle-women" who
cannot sew; thirty thousand of these latter now on the
pavements of London), and the kindred phenomena on
every hand: but it will be long before the fool of a
world open its eyes to the taproot of all that,—to the
fond notion, in short, That servantship and master-
ship, on the nomadic principle, was ever, or will ever
be, except for brief periods, possible among human
creatures.   Poor souls, and when they have discovered
it, what a puddling and weltering, and scolding and
jargoning, there will be, before the first real step towards remedy is taken !

Servantship, like all solid contracts between men
(like wedlock itself, which was *once* nomadic enough,
temporary enough!), must become a contract of per-
manency, not easy to dissolve, but difficult extremely,—
a " contract for life," if you can manage it (which you
cannot, without many wise laws and regulations, and a

great deal of earnest thought and anxious experience), will evidently be the best of all. And this was already the Nigger's essential position. Mischief, irregularities, injustices did probably abound between Nigger and Buckra; but the poisonous taproot of all mischief, and impossibility of fairness, humanity, or well-doing in the contract, never had been there! Of all else the remedy was easy in comparison; vitally important to every just man concerned in it; and, under all obstructions (which in the American case, begirt with frantic "Abolitionists," fire-breathing like the old Chimæra, were immense), was gradually getting itself done. To me individually the Nigger's case was not the most pressing in the world, but among the least so! America, however, had got into *Swarmery* upon it (not America's blame either, but in great part ours, and that of the nonsense *we* sent over to them); and felt that in the Heavens or the Earth there was nothing so godlike, or incomparably pressing to be done. Their energy, their valour, their &c. &c. were worthy of the stock they sprang from:—and now, poor fellows, *done* it they have, with a witness. A continent of the earth has been submerged, for certain years, by deluges as from the Pit of Hell; half a million (some say a whole million, but surely they exaggerate[1]) of excellent White Men, full of gifts and faculty, have torn and slashed one another into horrid death, in a temporary humour, which will leave centuries of remembrance fierce enough: and three million absurd Blacks, men and brothers (of a sort), are completely "emancipated;" launched into the career of improvement,—likely to be 'improved off the face of the earth' in a generation or

[1] 'More than half a million.' (Lunt, *Origin of the late War:* New York, 1867.)

two! That is the dismal prediction to me, of the warmest enthusiast to their Cause whom I have known of American men,—who doesn't regret his great efforts either, in the great Cause now won, Cause incomparably the most important on Earth or in Heaven at this time. *Papae, papae;* wonderful indeed!

In our own country, too, *Swarmery* has played a great part for many years past; and especially is now playing, in these very days and months. Our accepted axioms about "Liberty," "Constitutional Government," "Reform," and the like objects, are of truly wonderful texture: venerable by antiquity, many of them, and written in all manner of Canonical Books; or else, the newer part of them, celestially clear as perfect unanimity of all tongues, and *Vox populi vox Dei,* can make them: axioms confessed, or even inspirations and gospel verities, to the general mind of man. To the mind of here and there a man, it begins to be suspected that perhaps they are only conditionally true; that taken unconditionally, or under changed conditions, they are not true, but false and even disastrously and fatally so. Ask yourself about "Liberty," for example; what you do really mean by it, what in any just and rational soul is that Divine quality of liberty? That a good man be "free," as we call it, be permitted to unfold himself in works of goodness and nobleness, is surely a blessing to him, immense and indispensable;—to him and to those about him. But that a bad man be "free,"—permitted to unfold himself in *his* particular way, is contrariwise the fatallest curse you could inflict on him; curse and nothing else, to him and all his neighbours. Him the very Heavens call upon you to persuade, to urge, induce, compel, into something of well-doing; if you absolutely cannot, if he will continue in ill-doing,—then for him (I can assure you, though you will be shocked to hear it), the one "blessing" left is the speediest gallows you can lead him to. Speediest, that at least his ill-doing may cease *quàm primùm*. Oh, my friends, whither are you buzzing and swarming, in this extremely absurd manner? Expecting a Millennium from "extension of the suffrage," laterally, vertically, or in whatever way?

All the Millenniums I ever heard of heretofore were to be preceded by a "chaining of the Devil for a thousand years,"—laying *him* up, tied neck and heels, and put beyond stirring, as the preliminary. You too have been taking preliminary steps, with more and more ardour, for a thirty years back; but they seem to be all in the opposite direction: a cutting asunder of straps and ties, wherever you might find them; pretty indiscriminate of choice in the matter: a general repeal of old regulations, fetters, and restrictions (restrictions on the Devil originally, I believe, for most part, but now fallen slack and ineffectual), which had become unpleasant to many of you,—with loud shouting from the multitude, as strap after strap was cut, "Glory, glory, another strap is gone!"—this, I think, has mainly been the sublime legislative industry of Parliament since it became "Reform Parliament;" victoriously successful, and thought sublime and beneficent by some. So that now hardly any limb of the Devil has a thrum, or tatter of rope or leather left upon it:—there needs almost superhuman heroism in you to "whip" a garotter; no Fenian taken with the reddest hand is to be meddled with, under penalties; hardly a murderer, never so detestable and hideous, but you find him "insane," and board him at the public expense, a very

peculiar *British* Prytaneum of these days! And in fact,
THE DEVIL (he, verily, if you will consider the sense
of words) is likewise become an Emancipated Gentleman; lithe of limb, as in Adam and Eve's time, and
scarcely a toe or finger of him *tied* any more. And
you, my astonishing friends, *you* are certainly getting
into a millennium, such as never was before,—hardly
even in the dreams of Bedlam. Better luck to you by
the *way*, my poor friends; — a little less of buzzing,
humming, *swarming* (*i. e.* tumbling in infinite noise and
darkness), that you might try to look a little, each for
himself, what kind of " way" it is!

But indeed your " Reform" movement, from of old,
has been wonderful to me; everybody meaning by it,
not 'Reformation,' practical amendment of his own foul
courses, or even of his neighbour's, which is always
much welcomer; no thought of that whatever, though
that, you would say, is the one thing to be thought of
and aimed at;—but meaning simply "Extension of
the Suffrage." Bring in more voting; that will clear
away the universal rottenness, and quagmire of men-
dacities, in which poor England is drowning; let England only vote sufficiently, and all is clean and sweet
again. A very singular *swarmery* this of the Reform
movement, I must say.

III.

Inexpressibly delirious seems to me, at present in
my solitude, the puddle of Parliament and Public upon
what it calls the " Reform Measure;" that is to say,
The calling in of new supplies of blockheadism, gulli-
bility, bribeability, amenability to beer and balderdash,
by way of amending the woes we have had from our

previous supplies of that bad article. The intellect of a
man who believes in the possibility of "improvement"
by such a method is to me a finished off and shut up
intellect, with which I would not argue : mere waste of
wind between us to exchange words on that class of
topics. It is not Thought, this which my reforming
brother utters to me with such emphasis and eloquence;
it is mere 'reflex and reverberation,' repetition of what
he has always heard others imagining to think, and
repeating as orthodox, indisputable, and the gospel of
our salvation in this world. Does not all Nature groan
everywhere, and lie in bondage, till you give it a Parliament? Is one a man at all unless one have a suffrage to Parliament?   These are axioms admitted by
all English creatures for the last two hundred years.
If you have the misfortune not to believe in them at
all, but to believe the contrary for a long time past, the
inferences and inspirations drawn from them, and the
'*swarmeries*' and enthusiasms of mankind thereon, will
seem to you not a little marvellous!—

Meanwhile the *good* that lies in this delirious "new
Reform Measure,"—as there lies something of good in
almost everything,—is perhaps not inconsiderable.   It
accelerates notably what I have long looked upon as
inevitable;—pushes us at once into the Niagara Rapids :
irresistibly propelled, with ever - increasing velocity,
we shall now arrive; who knows how *soon!* For a
generation past, it has been growing more and more
evident that there was only this issue; but now the
issue itself has become imminent, the distance of it to
be guessed by years. Traitorous Politicians, grasping
at votes, even votes from the rabble, have brought it
on;—one cannot but consider them traitorous; and for

one's own poor share, would rather have been shot than been concerned in it. And yet, after all my silent indignation and disgust, I cannot pretend to be clearly sorry that such a consummation is expedited. I say to myself, "Well, perhaps the sooner such a mass of hypocrisies, universal mismanagements and brutal platitudes and infidelities *ends*,—if not in some improvement, then in death and finis,—may it not be the better? The sum of our sins, increasing steadily day by day, will at least be less, the sooner the settlement is!" Nay, have not I a kind of secret satisfaction, of the malicious or even of the judiciary kind (*schadenfreude*, 'mischief-joy,' the Germans call it, but really it is *justice*-joy withal), that he they call "Dizzy" is to do it; that other jugglers, of an unconscious and deeper type, having sold their poor Mother's body for a mess of Official Pottage, this clever conscious juggler steps in, " Soft you, my honourable friends; I will weigh out the corpse of your Mother (mother of mine she never was, but only stepmother and milk-cow);—and you sha'n't have the pottage: not yours, you observe, but mine!" This really is a pleasing trait of its sort. Other traits there are abundantly ludicrous, but they are too lugubrious to be even momentarily pleasant. A superlative Hebrew Conjuror, spell-binding all the great Lords, great Parties, great Interests of England, to his hand in this manner, and leading them by the nose, like helpless mesmerised somnambulant cattle, to such issue,—did the world ever see a *flebile ludibrium* of such magnitude before? Lath-sword, and Scissors of Destiny; Pickleherring and the Three *Parcœ* alike busy in it. This too, I suppose, we had deserved. The end of our poor Old England (such an England as we had at last made of it) to be not a tearful Tragedy, but an ignominious Farce as well!—

Perhaps the consummation may be now nearer than is thought. It seems to me sometimes as if everybody had privately now given up serious notion of resisting it. Beales and his ragamuffins pull down the railings of Her Majesty's Park, when Her Majesty refuses admittance; Home-Secretary Walpole (representing England's Majesty) listens to a Colonel Dickson talking of "barricades," "improvised pikes," &c.; does *not* order him to be conducted, and if necessary to be kicked, down stairs, with injunction never to return, in case of worse; and when Beales says, "I will see that the Queen's Peace is kept," Queen (by her Walpole) answers, "Will you, then; God bless *you!*" and bursts into tears. Those 'tears' are certainly an epoch in England; nothing seen, or dreamt of, like them in the History of poor England till now.

In the same direction we have also our remarkable " Jamaica Committee ;" and a Lord Chief Justice ' speaking six hours' (with such "eloquence," such &c. &c. as takes with ravishment the general Editorial ear, Penny and Threepenny), to prove that there is no such thing, nor ever was, as Martial Law ;—and that any governor, commanded soldier, or official person, putting down the frightfullest Mob-insurrection, Black or White, shall do it with the rope round *his* neck, by way of encouragement to him. Nobody answers this remarkable Lord Chief Justice, "Lordship, if you were to speak for six hundred years, instead of six hours, you would only prove the more to us that, unwritten if you will, but real and fundamental, anterior to all written laws and first making written laws *possible*, there must have been, and is, and will be, coeval with Human Society, from its first beginnings to its ultimate end, an actual *Martial Law*, of more validity than any other law whatever. Lordship, if there is no written law that three and three shall be six, do you wonder at the Statute-Book for that omission? You may shut those eloquent lips, and go home to dinner. May your shadow never be less; greater it perhaps has little chance of being."

Truly one knows not whether less to venerate the Majesty's Ministers, who, instead of rewarding their Governor Eyre, throw him out of window to a small loud group, small as now appears, and nothing but a group or knot of rabid Nigger-Philanthropists, barking furiously in the gutter, and threatening one's Reform Bill with loss of certain friends and votes (which could not save it, either, the dear object),—or that other unvenerable Majesty's Ministry, which, on Beales's generous undertaking for the Peace of an afflicted Queen's Majesty, bursts into tears.

Memorable considerably, and altogether new in our History, are both those ministerial feats; and both point significantly the same way. The perceptible, but as yet unacknowledged truth is, people are getting dimly sensible that our Social Affairs and Arrangements, all but the money-safe, are pretty universally a Falsehood, an elaborate old-established Hypocrisy, which is even serving its own poor private purpose ill, and is openly mismanaging every public purpose or interest, to a shameful and indefensible extent. For such a Hypocrisy, in any detail of it (except the money-safe), nobody, official or other, is willing to risk his skin; but cautiously looks round whether there is no postern to retire by, and retires accordingly,—leaving any mob-leader, Beales, John of Leyden, Walter the Penniless, or other impotent enough loud individual, with his tail of loud Roughs, to work their own sweet will. Safer to humour the mob than repress them, with the rope about *your* neck. Everybody sees this official slinking-off, has a secret fellow-feeling with it; nobody admires it; but the spoken disapproval is languid, and generally from the teeth outwards. " Has not everybody been very good to you ?" say the highest Editors, in these current days, admonishing and soothing down Beales and his Roughs.

So that, if loud mobs, supported by one or two Eloquences in the House, choose to proclaim, some day, with vociferation, as some day they will, " Enough of kingship, and its grimacings and futilities ! Is it not a Hypocrisy and Humbug, as you yourselves well know ? We demand to become *Commonwealth of England;* that will perhaps be better, worse it cannot be !"—in such case, how much of available resistance does the reader think would ensue ? From official persons, with the rope round their neck, should you expect a great amount ? I do not; or that resistance to the death would any-where, ' within these walls' or without, be the prevailing phenomenon.

For we are a people drowned in Hypocrisy; satu-rated with it to the bone:—alas, it is even so, in spite of far other intentions at one time, and of a languid, dumb, but ineradicable inward protest against it still: —and we are beginning to be universally conscious of that horrible condition, and by no means disposed to die in behalf of continuing it! It has lasted long, that unblessed process; process of 'lying to steep in the Devil's Pickle,' for above two hundred years (I date the formal beginning of it from the year 1660, and des-perate *return* of Sacred Majesty after such an ousting as it had got); process which appears to be now about complete. Who could regret the finis of such a thing; finis on any terms whatever! Possibly it will not be death eternal, possibly only death temporal, death temporary.

My neighbours, by the million against one, all expect that it will almost certainly be New-birth, a Saturnian time,—with gold nuggets themselves more plentiful than ever. As for us, we will say, Rejoice in the *awakening* of poor England even on these terms. To lie torpid, sluttishly gurgling and mumbling, spiritually in soak 'in the Devil's Pickle' (choicest elixir the Devil brews,—is not unconscious or half-conscious *Hypocrisy*, and quiet *Make-believe* of yourself and others, strictly that?) for above two hundred years: that was the infinitely dismal condition, all others are but finitely so.

IV.

Practically the worthiest inquiry, in regard to all this, would be: "What are probably the steps towards consummation all this will now take; what are, in main features, the issues it will arrive at, on unexpectedly (with immense surprise to the most) *shooting* Niagara, to the bottom? And above all, what are the possibilities, resources, impediments, conceivable methods and attemptings of its ever getting out again?" Darker subject of Prophecy can be laid before no man; and to be candid with myself, up to this date, I have never seriously meditated it, far less grappled with it as a Problem in any sort practical. Let me avoid branch *first* of this inquiry altogether. If 'immortal smash,' and shooting of the Falls, be the one issue ahead, our and the reformed Parliament's procedures and adventures in arriving there are not worth conjecturing, in comparison!—And yet the inquiry means withal, both branches if it mean, "What are the duties of good citizens in it, now and onwards ?" Meditated it must be, and light sought on it, however hard or impossible to find! It is not always the part of the infinitesimally small minority of wise men and good citizens to sit silent; idle they should never sit.

Supposing the *Commonwealth* established, and Democracy rampant, as in America, or in France by fits for 70 odd years past,—it is a favourable fact that our Aristocracy, in their essential height of position, and capability (or possibility) of doing good, are not at once likely to be interfered with; that they will be continued farther on their trial, and only the question somewhat more stringently put to them, "What *are* you good for, then ? Show us, show us, or else disappear!" I regard this as potentially a great benefit;—springing from what seems a mad enough phenomenon, the fervid zeal in *behalf* of this " new Reform Bill" and all kindred objects, which is manifested by the better kind of our young Lords and Honourables; a thing very curious to me. Somewhat resembling that bet of the impetuous Irish carpenter, astride of his plank firmly stuck out of window in the sixth story, " Two to one, I *can* saw this plank in so many minutes;" and sawing accordingly, fiercely impetuous,—with success! But from the maddest thing, as we said, there usually may come some particle of good withal (if any poor particle of *good* did lie in it, waiting to be disengaged!)—and this is a signal instance of that kind. Our Aristocracy are not hated or disliked by any Class of the People, but on the contrary are looked up to,—with a certain vulgarly human admiration, and spontaneous recognition of their good qualities and good fortune, which is by no means wholly envious or wholly servile,—by

C

all classes, lower and lowest class included. And indeed, in spite of lamentable exceptions too visible all round, my vote would still be, That from *Plebs* to *Princeps*, there was still no Class among us intrinsically so valuable and recommendable.

What the possibilities of our Aristocracy might still be? this is a question I have often asked myself. Surely their possibilities might still be considerable; though I confess they lie in a most abstruse, and as yet quite uninvestigated condition. But a body of brave men, and of beautiful polite women, furnished *gratis* as they are,—some of them (as my Lord Derby, I am told, in a few years will be) with not far from two-thirds of a million sterling annually,—ought to be good for something, in a society mostly fallen vulgar and chaotic like ours! More than once, I have been affected with a deep sorrow and respect for noble souls among them, and their high stoicism, and silent resignation to a kind of life which they individually could not alter, and saw to be so empty and paltry; life of giving and receiving Hospitalities in a gracefully splendid manner. "This, then" (such mute soliloquy I have read on some noble brow), "this, and something of Village-schools, of Consulting with the Parson, care of Peasant Cottages and Economies, is to be all our task in the world? Well, well; let us at least *do* this, in our most perfect way !"

In past years, I have sometimes thought what a thing it would be, could the Queen 'in Council' (in Parliament or wherever it were) pick out some gallant-minded, stout, well-gifted Cadet,—younger son of a Duke, of an Earl, of a Queen herself; younger Son doomed now to go mainly to the Devil, for absolute want of a career ;—and say to him, " Young fellow, if there do lie in you potentialities of governing, of gradually guiding, leading and coercing to a noble goal, how sad is it they should be all lost! They are the grandest gifts a mortal can have; and they are, of all, the most necessary to other mortals in this world. See, I have scores on scores of 'Colonies,' all ungoverned, and nine-tenths of them full of jungles, boa-constrictors, rattlesnakes, Parliamentary Eloquences, and Emancipated Niggers ripening towards nothing but destruction: one of these *you* shall have, you as Vice-King; on rational conditions, and *ad vitam aut culpam* it shall be yours (and perhaps your posterity's if worthy): go you and buckle with it, in the name of Heaven; and let us see what you will build it to!" To something how much better than the Parliamentary Eloquences are doing,—thinks the reader? Good Heavens, these West-India Islands, some of them, appear to be the richest and most favoured spots on the Planet Earth. Jamaica is an angry subject, and I am shy to speak of it. Poor Dominica itself is described to me in a way to kindle a heroic young heart; look at Dominica for an instant.

Hemispherical, they say, or in the shape of an Inverted Washbowl; rim of it, first twenty miles of it all round, starting from the sea, is flat alluvium, the fruitfullest in Nature, fit for any noblest spice or product, but unwholesome except for Niggers held steadily to their work: ground then gradually rises, umbrageously rich throughout, becomes fit for coffee; still rises, now bears oak woods, cereals, Indian corn, English wheat, and in this upper portion is salubrious and delightful for the European,—who might there spread and grow, according to the wisdom given him; say only to a population of 100,000 adult men; well fit to defend their Island against all comers, and beneficently keep steady

to their work a million of Niggers on the lower ranges.
What a kingdom my poor Friedrich Wilhelm, followed
by his Friedrich, would have made of this Inverted
Washbowl; clasped round, and lovingly kissed and laved
by the beautifullest seas in the world, and beshone by
the grandest sun and sky!

"Forever impossible," say you; "contrary to all
our notions, regulations and ways of proceeding or of
thinking?" Well, I daresay. And the state your regulations have it in, at present, is: Population of 100
white men (by no means of select type); unknown ci-
pher of rattlesnakes, profligate Niggers and Mulattoes;
governed by a Piebald Parliament of Eleven (head De-
mosthenes there a Nigger Tinman),—and so exquisite
a care of Being and of Well-being that the old Fortifi-
cations have become jungle-quarries (Tinman "at liberty
to tax himself"), vigorous roots penetrating the old ash-
lar, dislocating it everywhere, with tropical effect; old
cannon going quietly to honeycomb and oxide of iron,
in the vigorous embrace of jungle: military force nil,
police force next to nil: an Island capable of being
taken by the crew of a man-of-war's boat. And indeed
it was nearly lost, the other year, by an accidental col-
lision of two Niggers on the street, and a concourse of
other idle Niggers to see,—who would not go away
again, but idly re-assembled with increased numbers on
the morrow, and with ditto the next day; assemblage
pointing *ad infinitum* seemingly,—had not some charit-
able small French Governor, from his bit of Island
within reach, sent over a Lieutenant and twenty soldiers,
to extinguish the devouring absurdity, and order it home
straightway to its bed; which instantly saved this valuable Possession of ours, and left our Demosthenic Tinman and his Ten, with their liberty to tax themselves as

heretofore.　Is not "Self-government" a sublime thing, in Colonial Islands and some others? But to leave all this.

V.

I almost think, when once we have made the Niagara leap, the better kind of our Nobility, perhaps after experimenting, will more and more withdraw themselves from the Parliamentary, Oratorical or Political element; leaving that to such Cleon the Tanner and Company as it rightfully belongs to; and be far more chary of their speech than now.　Speech, issuing in no deed, is hateful and contemptible :—how can a man have any nobleness who knows not that?　In God's name, let us find out what of noble and profitable we can *do;* if it be nothing, let us at least keep silence, and bear gracefully our strange lot!—

The English Nobleman has still left in him, after such sorrowful erosions, something considerable of chivalry and magnanimity: polite he is, in the finest form; politeness, modest, simple, veritable, ineradicable, dwells in him to the bone; I incline to call him the politest kind of nobleman or man (especially his wife the politest and gracefullest kind of woman) you will find in any country.　An immense endowment this, if you consider it well!　A very great and indispensable help to whatever other faculties of *kingship* a man may have.　Indeed it springs from them all (its sources, every kingly faculty lying in you); and is as the beautiful natural skin, and visible sanction, index, and outcome of them all.　No king can rule without it; none but potential kings can really have it.　In the crude, what we call unbred or *Orson* form, all 'men of genius' have it; but see what it avails some of them,—your Samuel Johnson,

for instance,—in that crude form, who was so rich in it,
too, in the crude way!

Withal it is perhaps a fortunate circumstance, that
the population has no wild notions, no political enthusiasms of a "New Era" or the like. This, though in
itself a dreary and ignoble item, in respect of the revolutionary Many, may nevertheless be for good, if the
Few *shall* be really high and brave, as things roll on.

Certain it is, there is nothing but vulgarity in our
People's expectations, resolutions or desires, in this
Epoch. It is all a peaceable mouldering or tumbling
down from mere rottenness and decay; whether slowly
mouldering or rapidly tumbling, there will be nothing
found of real or true in the rubbish-heap, but a most
true desire of making money easily, and of eating it
pleasantly. A poor ideal for "reformers," sure enough.
But it is the fruit of long antecedents, too; and from of
old, our habits in regard to "reformation," or repairing
what went wrong (as something is always doing), have
been strangely didactic!

And to such length have we at last brought it, by
our wilful, conscious and now long-continued method of
using *varnish*, instead of actual repair by honest *car-
pentry*, of what we all knew and saw to have gone un-
deniably wrong in our procedures and affairs! Method
deliberately, steadily, and even solemnly continued, with
much admiration of it from ourselves and others, as the
best and only good one, for above two hundred years.
Ever since that *annus mirabilis* of 1660, when Oliver
Cromwell's dead clay was hung on the gibbet, and a
much easier "reign of Christ" under the divine gentleman called Charles II. was thought the fit thing, this
has been our steady method : varnish, varnish; if a thing

have grown so rotten that it yawns palpable, and is so inexpressibly ugly that the eyes of the very populace discern it and detest it,—bring out a new pot of varnish, with the requisite supply of putty; and lay it on handsomely. Don't spare varnish; how well it will all look in a few days, if laid on well! Varnish alone is cheap and is safe; avoid carpentering, chiselling, sawing and hammering on the old quiet House;—dry-rot is in it, who knows how deep; don't disturb the old beams and junctures: varnish, varnish, if you will be blessed by gods and men! This is called the Constitutional System, Conservative System, and other fine names; and this at last has its fruits,—such as we see. Mendacity hanging in the very air we breathe; all men become, unconsciously or half or wholly consciously, *liars* to their own souls and to other men's; grimacing, finessing, periphrasing, in continual hypocrisy of *word*, by way of varnish to continual past, present, future misperformance of *thing*:—clearly sincere about nothing whatever, except in silence, about the appetites of their own huge belly, and the readiest method of assuaging these. From a Population of that sunk kind, ardent only in pursuits that are low and in industries that are sensuous and *beaverish*, there is little peril of *human* enthusiasms, or revolutionary transports, such as occurred in 1789, for instance. A low-minded *pecus* all that; essentially torpid and *ignavum*, on all that is high or nobly human in revolutions.

It is true there is in such a population, of itself, no *help* at all towards reconstruction of the wreck of your Niagara plunge; of themselves they, with whatever cry of "liberty" in their mouths, are inexorably marked by Destiny as *slaves*; and not even the immortal gods could make them free,—except by making them anew and on a different pattern. No help in them at all, to your model Aristocrat, or to any noble man or thing. But then likewise there is no hindrance, or a minimum of it! Nothing there in *bar* of the noble Few, who we always trust will be born to us, generation after generation; and on whom and whose living of a noble and valiantly cosmic life amid the worst impediments and hugest anarchies, the whole of our hope depends. Yes, on them only! If amid the thickest welter of surrounding gluttony and baseness, and what must be reckoned bottomless anarchy from shore to shore, there be found no man, no small but invincible minority of men, capable of keeping themselves free from all that, and of living a heroically human life, while the millions round them are noisily living a mere beaverish or doglike one, then truly all hope is gone. But we always struggle to believe Not. Aristocracy by title, by fortune and position, who can doubt but there are still precious possibilities among the chosen of that class? And if that fail us, there is still, we hope, the unclassed Aristocracy by nature, not inconsiderable in numbers, and supreme in faculty, in wisdom, human talent, nobleness and courage, ' who derive their patent of nobility direct from Almighty God.' If indeed these also fail us, and are trodden out under the unanimous torrent of brutish hoofs and hobnails, and cannot vindicate themselves into clearness here and there, but at length cease even to try it,—then indeed it is all ended: national death, scandalous ' Copper-Captaincy' as of France, stern Russian Abolition and Erasure as of Poland; in one form or another, well deserved annihilation, and dismissal from God's universe, that and nothing else lies ahead for our once heroic England too.

How many of our Titular Aristocracy will prove

real gold when thrown into the crucible? That is
always a highly interesting question to me; and my
answer, or guess, has still something considerable of
hope lurking in it. But the question as to our Aristocracy by Patent from God the Maker, is infinitely interesting. How many of these, amid the ever-increasing
bewilderments, and welter of impediments, will be able
to develop themselves into something of Heroic Well-
doing by act and by word? How many of them will be
drawn, pushed and seduced, their very docility and lov-
ingness assisting, into the universal vulgar whirlpool of
Parliamenteering, Newspapering, Novel-writing, Comte-
Philosophy-ing, immortal Verse-writing, &c. &c. (if of
vocal turn, as they mostly will be, for some time yet)?
How many, by their too desperate resistance to the
unanimous vulgar of a Public round them, will become
spasmodic instead of strong; and will be overset, and
trodden out, under the hoofs and hobnails above-said?
Will there, in short, prove to be a recognisable small
nucleus of Invincible Ἄριστοι fighting for the Good
Cause, in their various wisest ways, and never ceasing
or slackening till they die? This is the question of
questions, on which all turns; in the answer to this,
could we give it clearly, as no man can, lies the oracle-
response, " Life for you," "Death for you"! Looking
into this, there are fearful dubitations many. But considering what of Piety, the devoutest and the bravest
yet known, there once was in England, and how exten-
sively, in stupid, maundering and degraded forms, it still
lingers, one is inclined timidly to hope the best!

The *best:* for if this small Aristocratic nucleus can
hold out and work, it is in the sure case to increase and
increase; to become (as Oliver once termed them) "a
company of poor men, who will spend all their blood

rather." An openly belligerent company, capable at last of taking the biggest slave Nation by the beard, and saying to it, "Enough, ye slaves, and servants of the mud-gods; all this must cease! Our heart abhors all this; our soul is sick under it; God's curse is on us while this lasts. Behold, we will all die rather than that this last. Rather all die, we say;—what is your view of the corresponding alternative on your own part?" I see well it must at length come to battle; actual fighting, bloody wrestling, and a great deal of it: but were it unit against thousand, or against thousand-thousand, on the above terms, I know the issue, and have no fear about it. That also is an issue which has been often tried in Human History; and, 'while God lives'—(I hope the phrase is not yet obsolete, for the fact is eternal, though so many have forgotten it!)—said issue can or will fall only one way.

VI.

What we can expect this Aristocracy of Nature to do for us? They are of two kinds: the Speculative, speaking or vocal; and the Practical or industrial, whose function is silent. These are of brother quality; but they go very different roads: 'men of *genius*' they all emphatically are, the 'inspired Gift of God' lodged in each of them. They do infinitely concern the world and us; especially that first or speaking class,—provided God *have* 'touched their lips with his hallowed fire'! Supreme is the importance of these. They are our inspired speakers and seers, the light of the world; who are to deliver the world from its swarmeries, its superstitions (*political* or other);—priceless and indispensable to us that first Class!

Nevertheless it is not of these I mean to speak at
present; the topic is far too wide, nor is the call to it
so immediately pressing. These Sons of Wisdom, gifted
to speak as with hallowed lips a real God's-message to
us,—I don't much expect they will be numerous, for a
long while yet, nor even perhaps appear at all in this
time of swarmeries, or be disposed to speak their mess-
age to such audience as there is. And if they did, I
know well it is not from my advice, or any mortal's,
that they could learn their feasible way of doing it.
For a great while yet, most of them will fly off into
" Literature," into what they call Art, Poetry and the
like; and will mainly waste themselves in that inane
region,—fallen so inane in our mad era. Alas, though
born Sons of Wisdom, they are not exempt from all our
' Swarmeries,' but only from the grosser kinds of them.
This of "Art," " Poetry" and so forth, is a refined Swarmery; the most refined now going; and comes to us, in
venerable form, from a distance of above a thousand
years. And is still undoubtingly sanctioned, canonised
and marked sacred, by the unanimous vote of cultivated
persons to this hour. How stir such questions in the
present limits? Or in fact, what chance is there that a
guess of mine, in regard to what these born Sons of
Wisdom in a yet unborn section of Time will say, or to
how they will say it, should avail in the least my own
contemporaries, much less them or theirs? Merely on
a point or two I will hint what my poor wish is; and
know well enough that it is the drawing a bow, not at
a venture indeed, but into the almost utterly dark.

First, then, with regard to Art, Poetry and the like,
which at present is esteemed the supreme of aims for
vocal genius, I hope my literary *Aristos* will pause, and
seriously make question before embarking on that; and

perhaps will end, in spite of the Swarmeries abroad, by
devoting his divine faculty to something far higher, far
more vital to us. Poetry? It is not pleasant singing
that we want, but wise and earnest speaking :—'Art,'
'High Art' &c. are very fine and ornamental, but only
to persons sitting at their ease : to persons still wrestling with deadly chaos, and still fighting for dubious
existence, they are a mockery rather. Our Aristos, well
meditating, will perhaps discover that the genuine 'Art'
in all times is a higher synonym for God Almighty's
Facts,—which come to us direct from Heaven, but in
so abstruse a condition, and cannot be read at all, till
the better intellect interpret them. That is the real
function of our Aristos and of his divine gift. Let him
think well of this ! He will find that all real 'Art' is
definable as Fact, or say as the disimprisoned 'Soul of
Fact;' that any other kind of Art, Poetry or High
Art is quite idle in comparison.

The *Bible* itself has, in all changes of theory about
it, this as its highest distinction, that it is the *truest* of
all Books ;—Book springing, every word of it, from the
intensest convictions, from the very heart's core, of those
who penned it. And has not that been a "successful"
Book? Did all the Paternoster-Rows of the world ever
hear of one so "successful"! Homer's *Iliad*, too, that
great Bundle of old Greek Ballads, is nothing of a *Fiction;* it is the *truest* a Patriotic Balladsinger, rapt into
paroxysm and enthusiasm for the honour of his native
Country and native Parish, could manage to sing. To
'sing,' you will observe; always sings,—pipe often rusty,
at a loss for metre (flinging-in his γε, μὲν, δὲ); a rough,
laborious, wallet-bearing man ; but with his heart rightly
on fire, when the audience goes with him, and 'hangs
on him with greed' (as he says they often do). Homer's

Iliad I almost reckon next to the *Bible;* so stubbornly sincere is it too, though in a far different element, and a far shallower.

"Fiction,"—my friend, you will be surprised to discover at last what alarming cousinship *it* has to *Lying:* don't go into "Fiction," you *Aristos,* nor concern yourself with "Fine Literature," or Coarse ditto, or the unspeakable glories and rewards of pleasing your generation; which you are not sent hither to *please,* first of all! In general, leave "Literature," the thing called "Literature" at present, to run through its rapid fermentations (how more and more rapid they are in these years!), and to fluff itself off into Nothing, in its own way,—like a poor bottle of soda-water with the cork sprung;—it won't be long. In our time it has become all the rage; highest noblemen and dignitaries courting a new still higher glory there; innumerable men, women and children rushing towards it, yearly ever more. It sat painfully in Grub Street, in hungry garrets, so long; some few heroic martyrs always serving in it, among such a miscellany of semi-fatuous worthless ditto, courting the bubble reputation in *worse* than the cannon's mouth; in general, a very flimsy, foolish set. But that little company of martyrs has at last lifted Literature furiously or foamingly high in the world. Goes like the Iceland geysers in our time,—like uncorked soda-water;—and will, as I said, soon have done. Only wait: in fifty years, I should guess, all really serious souls will have quitted that mad province, left it to the roaring populaces; and for any *Noble*-man or useful person it will be a credit rather to declare, "I never tried Literature; believe me, I have not written anything;"—and we of "Literature" by trade, we shall sink again, I perceive, to the rank of street-fiddling; no

higher rank, though with endless increase of sixpences
flung into the hat. Of "Literature" keep well to wind-
ward, my serious friend!—

"But is not Shakspeare the highest genius?" Yes,
of all the Intellects of Mankind that have taken the
speaking shape, I incline to think him the most divinely
gifted; clear, all-piercing like the sunlight, lovingly
melodious; probably the noblest human Intellect in that
kind. And yet of Shakspeare too, it is not the Fiction
that I admire, but the Fact; to say truth, what I most
of all admire are the traces he shows of a talent that
could have turned the *History of England* into a kind of
Iliad, almost perhaps into a kind of *Bible*. Manifest
traces that way; something of *epic* in the cycle of hasty
Fragments he has yielded us (slaving for his bread in
the Bankside Theatre);—and what a work wouldn't
that have been! Marlborough said, He knew no English History but what he had got from Shakspeare;
—and truly that is still essentially the serious and sad
fact for most of us; Fact thrice and four times lamentable, though Marlborough meant it lightly. Innumerable grave Books there are ; but for none of us
any real *History* of England, intelligible, profitable, or
even conceivable in almost any section of it !

To write the History of England as a kind of BIBLE
(or in parts and snatches, to *sing* it if you could), this
were work for the highest Aristos or series of Aristoi in
Sacred Literature (really a sacred kind, this); and to
be candid, I discover hitherto no incipiences of this;
and greatly desire that there were some ! Some I do expect (too fondly perhaps, but they seem to me a *sine
quâ non*) from the Writing and Teaching Heroes that
will yet be born to us. For England too (equally with
any Judah whatsoever) has a History that is Divine;

an Eternal Providence presiding over every step of it,
now in sunshine and soft tones, now in thunder and
storm, audible to millions of awe-struck valiant hearts
in the ages that are gone; guiding England forward
to *its* goal and work, which too has been highly considerable in the world! The "interpretation" of all
which, in the present ages, has (what is the root of all
our woes) fallen into such a set of hands! Interpretation scandalously ape-like, I must say; impious, blas-
phemous;—totally incredible withal. Which Interpretation will have to become pious and human again, or
else—or else vanish into the Bottomless Pit, and carry
us and our England along with it! This, some incipiences of this, I gradually expect from the Heroes that
are coming. And in fact *this*, taken in full compass, is
the one thing needed from them; and all other things
are but branches of this.

For example, I expect, as almost the first thing,
new definitions of LIBERTY from them; gradual extinc-
tion, slow but steady, of the stupid '*swarmeries*' of mankind on this matter, and at length a complete change
of their notions on it. 'Superstition and idolatry,' sins
real and grievous, sins ultimately ruinous, wherever
found,—this is now our English, our Modern European
form of them; Political, not Theological now! England, Modern Europe, will have to quit them or die.
They are sins of a fatal slow-poisonous nature; not permitted in this Universe. The poison of them is not intel-
lectual dimness chiefly, but torpid unveracity of heart:
not mistake of road, but want of pious earnestness in
seeking your road. Insincerity, unfaithfulness, impiety:
—careless tumbling and buzzing about, in blind, noisy,
pleasantly companionable 'swarms,' instead of solitary
questioning of yourself and of the Silent Oracles, which

is a sad, sore and painful duty, though a much incumbent
one , upon a man. The meaning of LIBERTY, what it
veritably signifies in the speech of men and gods, will
gradually begin to appear again? Were that once
got, the eye of England were *couched;* poor honest
England would again *see,*—I will fancy with what
horror and amazement,—the thing she had grown to in
this interim of *swarmeries.* To show this poor well-
meaning England, Whom it were desirable to furnish
with a "suffrage," and Whom with a *dog-muzzle* (and
plenty of fresh water on the streets), against rabidity in
the hot weather:—what a work for our Hero speakers
that are coming!—

I hope also they will attack earnestly, and at length
extinguish and eradicate, this idle habit of "accounting
for the Moral Sense," as they phrase it. A most singular problem:—instead of bending every thought to
have more and ever more of "Moral Sense," and there-
with to irradiate your own poor soul, and all its work,
into something of divineness, as the one thing needful
to you in this world! A very futile problem that other,
my friends; futile, idle, and far worse; leading to what
Moral *Ruin,* you little dream of! The Moral Sense,
thank God, is a thing you never will "account for;"
that, if you could think of it, is the perennial Miracle of
Man; in all times, visibly connecting poor transitory
Man here on this bewildered Earth with his Maker
who is Eternal in the Heavens. By no Greatest Hap-
piness Principle, Greatest Nobleness Principle, or any
Principle whatever, will you make that in the least
clearer than it already is;—forbear, I say; or you may
darken it away from you altogether! 'Two things,' says
the memorable Kant, deepest and most logical of Meta-
physical Thinkers, 'Two things strike me dumb: the

'infinite Starry Heaven; and the Sense of Right and
'Wrong in Man.' *Visible* Infinites, both; *say* nothing
of them; don't try to "account for them;" for you can
say nothing wise.

On the whole, I hope our Hero will, by heroic word,
and heroic thought and *act*, make manifest to mankind
that 'Reverence for God and for Man' is not yet extinct,
but only fallen into disastrous comatose sleep, and hide-
ously dreaming; that the 'Christian Religion itself is not
dead,' that the soul of it is alive forevermore,—and only
the dead and rotting *body* of it is now getting burial. The
noblest of modern Intellects, by far the noblest we have
had since Shakspeare left us, has said of this Religion;
'It is a Height to which the HUMAN SPECIES were fitted
'and destined to attain; and from which, having once
'attained it, they can never retrograde.' Permanently,
never. Never, *they;*—though individual Nations of
them fatally *can;* of which I hope poor England is not
one? Though, here as elsewhere, the *burial*-process does
offer ghastly enough phenomena: Ritualisms, Puseyisms,
Arches-Court Lawsuits, Cardinals of Westminster, &c.
&c.;—making night hideous! For a time and times
and half a time, as the old Prophets used to say.

One of my hoping friends, yet more sanguine than I
fully dare to be, has these zealous or enthusiast words:
'A very great "work," surely, is going on in these days,
'—has been *begun*, and is silently proceeding, and cannot
'easily *stop*, under all the flying dungheaps of this new
'"Battle of the Giants" flinging their *Dung*-Pelion on
'their Dung-Ossa, in these ballot-boxing, Nigger-eman-
'cipating, empty, dirt-eclipsed days:—no less a "work"
'than that of restoring GOD and whatever was Godlike
'in the traditions and recorded doings of Mankind;

' dolefully forgotten, or sham-remembered, as it has
' been, for long degraded and degrading hundreds of
' years, latterly ! Actually this, if you understand it well.
' The essential, still awful and ever-blessed Fact of all
' that was meant by "God and the Godlike" to men's souls
' is again struggling to become clearly revealed; will
' extricate itself from what some of us, too irreverently
' in our impatience, call "Hebrew old-clothes;" and will
' again bless the Nations; and heal them from their
' basenesses, and unendurable woes, and wanderings in
' the company of madness! This Fact lodges, not ex-
' clusively or specially in Hebrew Garnitures, Old or
' New; but in the Heart of Nature and of Man for-
' evermore. And is not less certain, here at this hour,
' than it ever was at any Sinai whatsoever. Kant's
' "Two things that strike me *dumb;*"—these are per-
' ceptible at Königsberg in Prussia, or at Charing-cross
' in London. And all eyes shall yet see them *better;*
' and the heroic Few, who are the salt of the earth, shall
' at length see them *well.* With results for everybody.
' A great "work" indeed; the greatness of which beg-
' gars all others !'

VII.

Of the second, or silent Industrial Hero, I may now
say something, as more within my limits and the reader's.

This Industrial hero, here and there recognisable
and known to me, as developing himself, and as an opulent and dignified kind of man, is already almost an
Aristocrat by class. And if his chivalry is still somewhat in the *Orson* form, he is already by intermarriage
and otherwise coming into contact with the Aristocracy
by title; and by degrees will acquire the fit *Valentinism,*
and other more important advantages there. He cannot

do better than unite with this naturally noble kind of Aristocrat by title; the Industrial noble and this one are brothers born; called and impelled to coöperate and go together. Their united result is what we want from both. And the Noble of the Future,—if there be any such, as I well discern there must,—will have grown out of both. A new "Valentine;" and perhaps a considerably improved,—by such *re*contact with his wild Orson kinsman, and with the earnest veracities this latter has learned in the Woods and the Dens of Bears.

The Practical 'man of genius' will probably *not* be altogether absent from the Reformed Parliament:—his *Make-believe*, the vulgar millionaire (truly a "bloated" specimen, this!) is sure to be frequent there; and along with the multitude of *brass* guineas, it will be very salutary to have a *gold* one or two!—In or out of Parliament, our Practical hero will find no end of work ready for him. It is he that has to recivilise, out of its now utter savagery, the world of Industry;—think what a set of items: To change *nomadic* contract into *permanent;* to annihilate the soot and dirt and squalid horror now defacing this England, once so clean and comely while it was poor; matters sanitary (and that not to the *body* only) for his people; matters governmental for them; matters &c. &c.:—no want of work for this Hero, through a great many generations yet!

And indeed Reformed Parliament itself, with or without his presence, will, you would suppose, have to start at once upon the Industrial question and go quite deep into it. That of Trades Union, in quest of its "Four eights,"[1] with assassin pistol in its hand, will at

---

[1] "Eight hours to work, eight hours to play,
Eight hours to sleep, and eight shillings a day!"
(*Reformed Workman's Pisgah Song.*)

once urge itself on Reformed Parliament: and Reformed Parliament will give us Blue Books upon it, if nothing further. Nay, almost still more urgent, and what I could reckon,—as touching on our Ark of the Covenant, on sacred "Free Trade" itself,—to be the preliminary of all, there is the immense and universal question of *Cheap and Nasty*. Let me explain it a little.

"Cheap and nasty;" there is a pregnancy in that poor vulgar proverb, which I wish we better saw and valued! It is the rude indignant protest of human nature against a mischief which, in all times and places, haunts it or lies near it, and which never in any time or place was so like utterly overwhelming it as here and now. Understand, if you will consider it, that no good man did, or ever should, encourage "cheapness" at the ruinous expense of *unfitness*, which is always infidelity, and is dishonourable to a man. If I want an article, let it be genuine, at whatever price; if the price is too high for me, I will go without it, unequipped with it for the present,—I shall not have equipped myself with a hypocrisy, at any rate! This, if you will reflect, is primarily the rule of all purchasing and all producing men. They are not permitted to encourage, patronise, or in any form countenance the working, wearing or acting of Hypocrisies in this world. On the contrary, they are to hate all such with a perfect hatred; to do their best in extinguishing them as the poison of mankind. This is the temper for purchasers of work: how much more for that of doers and producers of it! Work, every one of you, like the Demiurgus or Eternal World-builder; work, none of you, like the Diabolus or Denier and Destroyer,—under penalties!

And now, if this is the fact, that you are not to purchase, to make or to vend any ware or product of the "cheap and nasty" genus, and cannot in any case do it without sin, and even treason against the Maker of you, —consider what a *quantity* of sin, of treason, petty and high, must be accumulating in poor England every day! It is certain as the National Debt; and what are all National money Debts, in comparison! Do you know the shop, sale-shop, workshop, industrial establishment temporal or spiritual, in broad England, where genuine work is to be had? I confess I hardly do; the more is my sorrow! For a whole Pandora's Box of evils lies in that one fact, my friend; that one is enough for us, and may be taken as the sad summary of all. Universal *shoddy* and Devil's-dust cunningly varnished over; that is what you will find presented you in all places, as ware invitingly cheap, if your experience is like mine. Yes; if Free Trade is the new religion, and if Free Trade do mean, Free racing with unlimited velocity in the career of *Cheap and Nasty*,—our Practical hero will be not a little anxious to deal with that question. Infinitely anxious to see how "Free Trade," with such a devil in the belly of it, is to be got *tied* again a little, and forbidden to make a very brute of itself at this rate!

Take one small example only. London bricks are reduced to dry clay again in the course of sixty years, or sooner. *Bricks*, burn them rightly, build them faithfully, with mortar faithfully tempered, they will stand, I believe, barring earthquakes and cannon, for 6,000 years if you like! Etruscan Pottery (*baked clay*, but rightly baked) is some 3,000 years of age, and still fresh as an infant. Nothing I know of is more lasting than a well-made brick,—we have them here, at the head of this Garden (wall once of a Manor Park), which are in

their third or fourth century (Henry Eighth's time, I
was told), and still perfect in every particular.

Truly the state of London houses and London house-
building, at this time, who shall express how detestable
it is, how frightful! "Not a house this of mine," said
one indignant gentleman, who had searched the London
Environs all around for any bit of Villa, "Alpha"-cot-
tage or Omega, which were less inhuman, but found
none: "Not a built house, but a congeries of plastered
bandboxes; shambling askew in all joints and corners
of it; creaking, quaking under every step;—filling you
with disgust and despair!" For there lies in it not
the Physical mischief only, but the Moral too, which
is far more. I have often sadly thought of this. That
a fresh human soul should be born in such a place;
born in the midst of a concrete mendacity; taught at
every moment not to abhor a lie, but to think a lie all
proper, the fixed custom and general law of man, and to
twine its young affections round that sort of object!

England needs to be *rebuilt* once every seventy years.
Build it once *rightly*, the expense will be, say fifty per
cent more; but it will stand till the Day of Judgment.
Every seventy years we shall save the expense of building all England over again! Say nine-tenths of the
expense, say three-fourths of it (allowing for the changes
necessary or permissible in the change of things); and
in rigorous arithmetic, such is the saving possible to
you; lying under your nose there; soliciting you to pick
it up,—by the mere act of behaving like sons of Adam,
and not like scandalous esurient Phantasms and sons of
Bel and the Dragon.

Here is a thrift of money, if you want money! The
money-saving would (you can compute in what short
length of time) pay your National Debt for you, bridge

the ocean for you; wipe away your smoky nuisances, your muddy ditto, your miscellaneous ditto, and make the face of England clean again;—and all this I reckon as mere zero in comparison with the accompanying improvement to your poor souls,—now dead in trespasses and sins, drowned in beer-buts, wine-butts, in gluttonies, slaveries, quackeries, but recalled *then* to blessed life again, and the sight of Heaven and Earth, instead of Payday, and Meux and Co.'s Entire. Oh, my bewildered Brothers, what foul infernal Circe has come over you, and changed you from men once really rather noble of their kind, into beavers, into hogs and asses, and beasts of the field or the slum! I declare I had rather die. . . .

One hears sometimes of religious controversies running very high; about faith, works, grace, prevenient grace, the Arches Court and *Essays and Reviews;*—into none of which do I enter, or concern myself with your entering. One thing I will remind you of, That the essence and outcome of all religions, creeds and liturgies whatsoever is, To do one's work in a faithful manner. Unhappy caitiff, what to you is the use of orthodoxy, if with every stroke of your hammer you are breaking all the Ten Commandments,—operating upon Devil's-dust, and with constant invocation of the Devil, endeavouring to reap where you have not sown?—

Truly, I think our Practical Aristos will address himself to this sad question, almost as the primary one of all. It is impossible that an Industry, national or personal, carried on under 'constant invocation of the Devil,' can be a blessed or happy one in any fibre or detail of it! Steadily, in every fibre of it, from heart to skin, that is and remains an Industry accursed;

nothing but bewilderment, contention, misery, mutual rage, and continually advancing ruin, *can* dwell there. *Cheap and Nasty* is not found on shop-counters alone; but goes down to the centre,—or indeed springs from it. Overend-Gurney Bankruptcies, Chatham-and-Dover Railway Financierings,—Railway "Promoters" generally (and no oakum or beating of hemp to give them, instead of that nefarious and pernicious industry) ;—Sheffield Sawgrinders and Assassination Company; "Four-eights," and workman's Pisgah Song: all these are diabolic short-cuts towards wages; clutchings at money without just work done; all these are *Cheap and Nasty* in another form. The glory of a workman, still more of a master-workman, That he does his work well, ought to be his most precious possession; like "the honour of a soldier," dearer to him than life. That is the ideal of the matter:—lying, alas, how far away from us at present! But if you yourself *demoralise* your soldier, and teach him continually to invoke the Evil Genius and to *dis*honour himself,—what do you expect your big Army will grow to?—

"The *prestige* of England. on the Continent," I am told, is much decayed of late; which is a lamentable thing to various Editors; to me not. '*Prestige, præstigium,* magical illusion,'—I never understood that poor England had in her good days, or cared to have, any "*prestige* on the Continent" or elsewhere; England was wont to follow her own affairs in a diligent heavy-laden frame of mind, and had an almost perfect stoicism as to what the Continent, and its extraneous ill-informed populations might be thinking of her. Nor is it yet of the least real importance what '*prestiges,* :magical illusions,' as to England, foolish neighbours may take up;

important only one thing, What England *is*. The account of that in Heaven's Chancery, I doubt, is very bad: but as to "*prestige*," I hope the heart of the poor Country would still say,—"Away with your *prestige;* that won't help me or hinder me! The word was Napoleonic, expressive enough of a Grand-Napoleonic fact: better leave it on its own side of the Channel; not wanted here!"

Nevertheless, unexpectedly, I have myself something to tell you about English *prestige.* "In my young "time," said lately to me one of the wisest and faithfullest German Friends I ever had, a correct observer, and much a lover both of his own country and of mine, "In my boyhood" (that is, some fifty years ago, in Würzburg country, and Central Germany), "when you "were going to a shop·to purchase, wise people would " advise you: 'If you can find an English article of " the sort wanted, buy that; it will be a few pence " dearer; but it will prove itself a well-made, faithful " and skilful thing; a comfortable servant and friend to " you for a long time; better buy that.' And now," continued he, "directly the reverse is the advice given : " 'If you find an English article, don't buy that; that " will be a few pence cheaper, but it will prove only a " more cunningly devised mendacity than any of the " others; avoid that above all.' Both were good ad- " vices; the former fifty years ago was a good advice; " the latter is now." Would to Heaven this were a *præstigium* or magical illusion only!—

But to return to our Aristocracy by title.

VIII.

Orsonism is not what will hinder our Aristocracy from still reigning, still, or much farther than now,—to the very utmost limit of their capabilities and opportunities, in the new times that come. What are these *opportunities*,—granting the capability to be (as I believe) very considerable if seriously exerted?—This is a question of the highest interest just now.

In their own Domains and land territories, it is evident each of them can still, for certain years and decades, be a complete king; and may, if he strenuously try, mould and manage everything, till both his people and his dominion correspond gradually to the ideal he has formed. Refractory subjects he has the means of *banishing;* the relations between all classes, from the biggest farmer to the poorest orphan ploughboy, are under his control; nothing ugly or unjust or improper, but he could by degrees undertake steady war against, and manfully subdue or extirpate. Till all his Domain were, through every field and homestead of it, and were maintained in continuing and being, manlike, decorous, fit; comely to the eye and to the soul of whoever wisely looked on it, or honestly lived in it. This is a beautiful ideal; which might be carried out on all sides to indefinite lengths,—not in management of land only, but in thousandfold countenancing, protecting and encouraging of human worth, and *dis*countenancing and sternly repressing the want of ditto, wherever met with among surrounding mankind. Till the whole surroundings of a nobleman were made noble like himself: and all men should recognise that here verily was a bit of kinghood ruling "by the Grace of God," in difficult circumstances, but *not* in vain.

This were a way, if this were commonly adopted, of by degrees reinstating Aristocracy in all the privileges, authorities, reverences and honours it ever had, in its palmiest times, under any Kaiser Barbarossa, Henry Fowler (*Heinrich der Vogler*), Henry Fine - Scholar (*Beau-clerc*), or Wilhelmus Bastardus the Acquirer: this would be divine; blessed is every individual that shall manfully, all his life, solitary or in fellowship, address himself to this! But, alas, this is an ideal, and I have practically little faith in it. Discerning well how *few* would seriously adopt this as a trade in life, I can only say, "Blessed is every one that does!"— Readers can observe that only zealous aspirants to *be* 'noble' and worthy of their title (who are not a numerous class) could adopt this trade; and that of these few, only the fewest, or the actually *noble*, could to much effect do it when adopted. 'Management of one's land on this principle,' yes, in some degree this might be possible: but as to 'fostering merit' or human worth, the question would arise (as it did with a late Noble Lord still in wide enough esteem),[1] "What is merit? The opinion one man entertains of another!" (*Hear, hear!*) By *this* plan of diligence in promoting human worth, you would do little to redress our griefs; this plan would be a quenching of the fire by oil: a dreadful plan! In fact, this is what you may see everywhere going on just now; this is what has reduced us to the pass we are at!—To recognise merit, you must first yourself have it; to recognise false merit, and crown it as true, because a long tail runs after it, is the saddest operation under the sun; and it is one you have only to open your eyes and see every day. Alas, no:

[1] Lord Palmerston, in debate on Civil-Service Examination Proposal.

Ideals won't carry many people far. ₍To have an Ideal generally done, it must be compelled by the vulgar appetite there is to do it, by indisputable advantage seen in doing it.

And yet, in such an independent position; acknowledged king of one's own territories, well withdrawn from the raging inanities of " politics," leaving the loud rabble and their spokesmen to consummate all that in their own sweet way, and make Anarchy again horrible, and Government or real Kingship the thing desirable,—one fancies there might be actual scope for a kingly soul to aim at unfolding itself, at imprinting itself in all manner of beneficent arrangements and improvements˙ of things around it.

Schools, for example, schooling and training of *its* young subjects in the way that they should go, and in the things that they should do : what a boundless outlook that of schools, and of improvement in school methods, and school purposes, which in these ages lie hitherto all superannuated and to a frightful degree inapplicable!   Our schools go all upon the *vocal* hitherto ; no clear aim in them but to teach the young creature how he is to *speak*, to utter himself by tongue and pen ;—which, supposing him even to *have something to utter*, as he so very rarely has, is by no means the thing he specially wants in our times.   How he is to work, to behave and do ; that is the question for him, which he seeks the answer of in schools ;—in schools, having now so little chance of it elsewhere.   In other times, many or most of his neighbours round him, his superiors over him, if he looked well and could take example, and learn by what he saw, were in use to yield him very much of answer to this vitallest of questions : but now they do not, or do it fatally the reverse way !   Talent

of speaking grows daily commoner among one's neighbours; amounts already to a weariness and a nuisance,
so barren is it of great benefit, and liable to be of great
hurt: but the talent of right conduct, of wise and useful behaviour seems to grow rarer every day, and is
nowhere taught in the streets and thoroughfares any
more. Right schools were never more desirable than
now. Nor ever more unattainable, by public clamor-
ing and jargoning, than now. Only the wise ·Ruler
(acknowledged king in his own territories), taking
counsel with the wise, and earnestly pushing and endeavouring all his days, might do something in it. It
is true, I suppose him to be capable of recognising and
searching out ' the *wise*,' who are apt *not* to be found
on the high roads at present, or only to be transiently
passing there, with closed lips, swift step, and possibly
a grimmish aspect of countenance, among the crowd of
loquacious *sham*-wise. To be capable of actually recognising and discerning these; and that is no small postulate (how great a one I know well):—in fact, unless
our Noble by rank be a Noble by nature, little or no
success is possible to us by him.

But granting this great postulate, what a field in
the *Non-vocal* School department, such as was not
dreamt of before! *Non-vocal;* presided over by whatever of Pious Wisdom this king could eliminate from
all corners of the impious world; and could consecrate
with means and appliances for making the new generation, by degrees, less impious. Tragical to think of:
Every new generation is born to us direct out of Heaven; white as purest writing-paper, white as snow;—
everything we please can be written on it;—and our
pleasure and our negligence is, To begin blotching it,
scrawling, smutching and smearing it, from the first

day it sees the sun; towards such a consummation of
ugliness, dirt and blackness of darkness, as is too often
visible.   Woe on us; there is no woe like this,—if we
were not sunk in stupefaction, and had still eyes to
discern or souls to feel it !—Goethe has shadowed out
a glorious far-glancing specimen of that Non-vocal, or
very partially-vocal kind of School.   I myself remem-
ber to have seen an extremely small, but highly useful
and practicable little corner of one, actually on work
at Glasnevin in Ireland about fifteen years ago; and
have often thought of it since.

IX.

I always fancy there might much be done in the
way of military Drill withal.   Beyond all other schooling, and as supplement or even as succedaneum for all
other, one often wishes the entire Population could be
thoroughly drilled; into coöperative movement, into
individual behaviour, correct, precise, and at once ha-
bitual and orderly as mathematics, in all or in very
many points,—and ultimately in the point of actual
Military Service, should such be required of it !

That of commanding and obeying, were there nothing more, is it not the basis of all human culture;
ought not all to have it; and how many ever do?   I
often say, The one Official Person, royal, sacerdotal,
scholastic, governmental, of our times, who is still
thoroughly a truth and a reality, and *not* in great part
a hypothesis, and worn-out humbug, proposing and
attempting a duty which he fails to do,—is the Drill-
Sergeant who is master of his work, and who will per-
form it.   By Drill-Sergeant understand, not the man
in three stripes alone; understand him as meaning all

such men, up to the Turenne, to the Friedrich of Prussia; *he* does his function, he is genuine; and from the highest to the lowest no one else does. Ask your poor King's Majesty, Captain-General of England, Defender of the Faith, and so much else; ask your poor Bishop, sacred Overseer of souls; your poor Lawyer, sacred Dispenser of justice; your poor Doctor, ditto of health : they will all answer, " Alas, no, worthy sir, we are all of us unfortunately fallen not a little, some of us altogether, into the imaginary or quasi-humbug condition, and cannot help ourselves; he alone of the three stripes, or of the gorget and baton, *does* what he pretends to !" That is the melancholy fact; well worth considering at present.—Nay, I often consider farther, If, in any Country, the Drill-Sergeant himself fall into the partly imaginary or humbug condition (as is my frightful apprehension of him here in England, on survey of him in his marvellous Crimean expeditions, marvellous Court-martial revelations, Newspaper controversies, and the like), what is to become of that Country and its thrice-miserable Drill-Sergeant? Reformed Parliament, I hear, has decided on a " thorough Army reform," as one of the first things. So that we shall at length have a perfect Army, field-worthy and correct in all points, thinks Reformed Parliament? Alas, yes;—and if the sky fall, we shall catch larks, too !—

But now, what is to hinder the acknowledged king in all corners of his territory, to introduce wisely a universal system of Drill, not military only, but human in all kinds; so that no child or man born in *his* territory might miss the benefit of it,—which would be immense to man, woman and child? I would begin with it, in mild, soft forms, so soon almost as my children were

able to stand on their legs; and I would never wholly
remit it till they had done with the world and me.
Poor Wilderspin knew something of this; the great
Goethe evidently knew a great deal! This of outwardly
combined and plainly consociated Discipline, in simultaneous movement and action, which may be practical,
symbolical, artistic, mechanical in all degrees and modes,
—is one of the noblest capabilities of man (most sadly un-
dervalued hitherto); and one he takes the greatest pleasure in exercising and unfolding, not to mention at all
the invaluable benefit it would afford him if unfolded.
From correct marching in line, to rhythmic dancing in
cotillon or minuet,—and to infinitely higher degrees
(that of symbolling in concert your " first reverence," for
instance, supposing reverence and symbol of it to be
both sincere!)—there is a natural charm in it; the fulfilment of a deep-seated, universal desire, to all rhythmic
social creatures! In man's heaven-born Docility, or
power of being Educated, it is estimable as perhaps the
deepest and richest element; or the next to that of
music, of Sensibility to Song, to Harmony and Number,
which some have reckoned the deepest of all. A richer
mine than any in California for poor human creatures;
richer by what a multiple; and hitherto as good as
never opened,—worked only for the Fighting purpose.
Assuredly I would not neglect the Fighting purpose;
no, from sixteen to sixty, not a son of mine but should
know the Soldier's function too, and be able to defend
his native soil and self, in best perfection, when need
came. But I should not begin with this; I should care-
fully end with this, after careful travel in innumerable
fruitful fields by the way leading to this.

It is strange to me, stupid creatures of routine as we
mostly are, how in all education of mankind, this of

simultaneous Drilling into combined rhythmic action, for almost all good purposes, has been overlooked and left neglected by the elaborate and many-sounding Pedagogues and Professorial persons we have had, for the long centuries past! It really should be set on foot a little; and developed gradually into the multiform opulent results it holds for us. As might well be done, by an acknowledged king in his own territory, if he were wise. To all children of men it is such an entertainment, when you set them to it. I believe the vulgarest Cockney crowd, flung out millionfold on a Whit-Monday, with nothing but beer and dull folly to depend on for amusement, would at once kindle into something human, if you set them to do almost any regulated act in common. And would dismiss their beer and dull foolery, in the silent charm of rhythmic human companionship, in the practical feeling, probably new, that all of us are made on one pattern, and are, in an unfathomable way, brothers to one another.

Soldier-Drill, for fighting purposes, as I have said, would be the last or finishing touch of all these sorts of Drilling; and certainly the acknowledged king would reckon it not the least important to him, but even perhaps the most so, in these peculiar times. Anarchic Parliaments and Penny Newspapers might perhaps grow jealous of him; in any case, he would have to be cautious, punctilious, severely correct, and obey to the letter whatever laws and regulations they emitted on the subject. But that done, how could the most anarchic Parliament, or Penny Editor, think of forbidding any fellow-citizen such a manifest improvement on all the human creatures round him? Our wise hero Aristocrat, or acknowledged king in his own territory, would by no

E

means think of employing his superlative private Field-regiment in levy of war against the most anarchic Parliament; but, on the contrary, might and would loyally help said Parliament in warring down much anarchy worse than its own, and so gain steadily new favour from it. From it, and from all men and gods! And would have silently the consciousness, too, that with every new Disciplined Man, he was widening the arena of *Anti*-Anarchy, of God-appointed *Order* in this world and Nation,—and was looking forward to a day, very distant probably, but certain as Fate.

For I suppose it would in no moment be doubtful to him that, between Anarchy and Anti-ditto, it would have to come to sheer fight at last; and that nothing short of duel to the death could ever void that great quarrel. And he would have his hopes, his assurances, as to how the victory would lie. For everywhere in this Universe, and in every Nation that is not *divorced* from it and in the act of perishing forever, Anti-Anarchy is silently on the increase, at all moments: Anarchy not, but contrariwise; having the whole Universe forever set against it; pushing *it* slowly, at all moments, towards suicide and annihilation. To Anarchy, however million-headed, there is no victory possible. Patience, silence, diligence, ye chosen of the world! Slowly or fast, in the course of time, you will grow to a minority that can actually step forth (sword not yet drawn, but sword ready to be drawn), and say: " Here are we, Sirs; we also are now minded to *vote*,—to all lengths, as you may perceive. A company of poor men (as friend Oliver termed us) who will spend all our blood, if needful!" What are Beales and his 50,000 roughs against such; what are the noisiest anarchic Parliaments, in majority of a million to one, against such? Stubble against fire. Fear not, my friend; the issue is very certain when it comes so far as this!

X.

These are a kind of enterprises, hypothetical as yet, but possible evidently more or less, and, in all degrees of them, tending towards noble benefit to oneself and to all one's fellow-creatures; which a man born noble by title and by nature, with ample territories and revenues, and a life to dispose of as he pleased, might go into, and win honour by, even in the England that now is. To my fancy, they are bright little potential breaks, and up-turnings, of that disastrous cloud which now overshadows his best capabilities and him;—as every blackest cloud in this world has withal a 'silver lining;' and is, full surely, beshone by the Heavenly lights, if we *can* get to that other side of it! More of such fine possibilities I might add: that of "Sanitary regulation," for example; To see the divinely-appointed laws and conditions of Health, at last, *humanly* appointed as well; year after year, more exactly ascertained, rendered valid, habitually practised, in one's own Dominion; and the old adjective 'Healthy' once more becoming synonymous with 'Holy,'—what a conquest there! But I forbear; feeling well enough how visionary these things look; and how aerial, high and spiritual they *are;* little capable of seriously tempting, even for moments, any but the highest kinds of men. Few Noble Lords, I may believe, will think of taking this course; indeed not many, as Noble Lords now are, could do much good in it. Dilettantism will avail nothing in any of these enterprises; the law of them is, grim labour, earnest and continual; certainty of many contradictions, disappointments; a life, not of ease and pleasure, but of noble and sorrowful toil; the reward of it far off,—fit only for heroes !

Much the readiest likelihood for our Aristocrat by title would be that of coalescing nobly with his two Brothers, the Aristocrats by nature, spoken of above. Both greatly need him; especially the Vocal or Teaching one, wandering now desolate enough, heard only as a *Vox Clamantis e Deserto ;*—though I suppose, it will be with the Silent or Industrial one, as with the easier of the two, that our Titular first comes into clear coöperation. This Practical hero, Aristocrat by nature, and standing face to face and hand to hand, all his days, in life-battle with practical Chaos (with dirt, disorder, nomadism, disobedience, folly and confusion), slowly coercing it into Cosmos, will surely be the natural ally for any titular Aristocrat who is bent on being a real one as the business of his life. No other field of activity is half so promising as the united field which those two might occupy. By nature and position they are visibly a kind of Kings, actual British 'Peers' (or Vice-Kings, in absence and abeyance of any visible King); and might take manifold counsel together, hold manifold 'Parliament' together (*Vox e Deserto* sitting there as 'Bench of Bishops,' possibly !)—and might mature and adjust innumerable things. Were there but three Aristocrats of each sort in the whole of Britain, what beneficent unreported '*Parliamenta*,'—actual human consultations and earnest deliberations, responsible to no "*Buncombe*," disturbed by no Penny Editor,—on what the whole Nine were earnest to see done ! By degrees, there would some beginnings of success and Cosmos be achieved upon this our unspeakable Chaos; by degrees something of

light, of prophetic twilight, would be shot across its
unfathomable dark of horrors,—prophetic of victory,
sure though far away.

Penny-Newspaper Parliaments cannot legislate on
anything; they know the real properties and qualities of no *thing*, and don't even try or want to know
them,—know only what *"Buncombe"* in its darkness
thinks of them. No law upon a *thing* can be made, on
such terms; nothing but a mock-law, which Nature
silently abrogates, the instant your third reading is done.
But men in contact with the fact, and earnestly questioning it, can at length ascertain what *is* the law of it,
—what it will behove any Parliament (of the Penny-
Newspaper sort or other) to enact upon it. Whole
crops and harvests of authentic "Laws," now pressingly needed and not obtainable, upon our new British
Industries, Interests and Social Relations, I could fancy
to be got into a state of forwardness, by small virtual
'Parliaments' of this unreported kind,—into a real state
of preparation for enactment by what actual Parliament there was, itself so incompetent for "legislating"
otherwise. These are fond dreams? Well, let us hope
not altogether. Most certain it is, an immense Body
of Laws upon these new Industrial, Commercial, Railway &c. Phenomena of ours are pressingly wanted; and
none of mortals knows where to get them. For example, the Rivers and running Streams of England; prim-
ordial elements of this our poor Birth-land, face-features
of it, created by Heaven itself : Is Industry free to tum-
ble out whatever horror of refuse it may have arrived at
into the nearest crystal brook ? Regardless of gods and
men and little fishes. Is Free Industry free to convert
all our rivers into Acherontic sewers; England generally
into a roaring sooty smith's forge? Are we all doomed

to eat dust, as the Old Serpent was, and to breathe solutions of soot? Can a Railway Company with "Promoters" manage, by *feeing* certain men in bombazeen, to burst through your bedroom in the night-watches, and miraculously set all your crockery jingling? Is an Englishman's house still his castle; and in what sense?—Examples plenty!

The Aristocracy, as a class, has as yet no thought of giving up the game, or ceasing to be what in the language of flattery is called "Governing Class;" nor should, till it have seen farther. In the better heads among them are doubtless grave misgivings; serious enough reflections rising,—perhaps not sorrowful altogether; for there must be questions withal, " Was it so very blessed a function, then, that of ' Governing' on the terms given?" But beyond doubt the vulgar Noble Lord intends fully to continue the game,—with doubly severe study of the new rules issued on it;—and will still, for a good while yet, go as heretofore into Electioneering, Parliamentary Engineering; and hope against hope to keep weltering atop by some method or other, and to make a fit existence for himself in that miserable old way. An existence filled with labour and anxiety, with disappointments and disgraces and futilities I can promise him, but with little or nothing else. Let us hope he will be wise to discern, and not continue the experiment too long!

He has lost his place in that element; nothing but services of a sordid and dishonourable nature, betrayal of his own Order, and of the noble interests of England, can gain him even momentary favour there. He cannot bridle the wild horse of a Plebs any longer:—for a generation past, he has not even tried to bridle it; but has run panting and trotting meanly by the side of it, pat-

ting its stupid neck; slavishly plunging with it into any
"Crimean" or other slough of black platitudes it might
reel towards,—anxious he, only not to be kicked away,
not just yet; oh, not yet for a little while! Is this an
existence for a man of any honour; for a man ambitious
of more honour? I should say, not. And he still thinks
to hang by the bridle, now when his Plebs is getting into
the gallop? Hanging by its bridle, through what steep
brambly places (scratching out the very *eyes* of him, as
is often enough observable), through what malodorous
quagmires, and ignominous pools, will the wild horse
drag him,—till he quit hold! Let him quit, in Heaven's name. Better he should go yachting to Algeria,
and shoot lions for an occupied existence (or stay at
home, and hunt rats; is not, in strict truth, the Rat-
catcher our one *real* British Nimrod now?)—Game pre-
serving, Highland deer-stalking and all that, will have
ceased in this over-crowded country; and I can see no
other business for the vulgar Noble Lord, if he will continue vulgar.

LONDON:

ROBSON AND SON, GREAT NORTHERN PRINTING WORKS,
PANCRAS ROAD, N.W.

Printed in the United Kingdom
by Lightning Source UK Ltd.
115567UKS00001B/211